evonne goolagong

by Charles and Ann Morse

illustrated by Harold Henriksen

Amecus Street
Mankato, Minnesota 56001

Published by Amecus Street, 123 South Broad Street, P. O. Box 113, Mankato, Minnesota 56001
Copyright © 1974 by Amecus Street. International copyrights reserved in all countries.
No part of this book may be reproduced in any form without written permission from the publisher.
Printed in the United States.
Distributed by Childrens Press, 1224 West Van Buren Street, Chicago, Illinois 60607
Library of Congress Number: 74-796   ISBN: 0-87191-339-9

Library of Congress Cataloging in Publication Data
Morse, Charles.   Evonne Goolagong.   (Superstars)
SUMMARY: Biography of the champion Australian tennis player of part Aboriginal heritage.
1. Goolagong, Evonne, 1951-   —Juvenile literature.
[1. Goolagong, Evonne, 1951-   2. Tennis—Biography]
I. Morse, Ann, joint author.   II. Henriksen, Harold, illus.   III. Title.
GV994.G67M67   796.34'2'0924   [B]   [92]   74-796   ISBN 0-87191-339-9

On the day of the 1971 women's final at Wimbledon, something unusual happened. A 19-year-old kid, Evonne Goolagong, put down her transistor radio and strolled onto Center Court. She was smiling. Someone near the court even thought he heard her humming. Smiling and humming. That was unheard of. At Wimbledon, you are supposed to look scared stiff. Your knees are supposed to feel like jelly. And you should look very serious. But Evonne was smiling, almost dancing, onto the smooth turf of the Center Court.

The part-Aboriginal Goolagong girl from a remote town in Australia took the All-England tennis crown away from the reigning queen. Evonne Goolagong upset Margaret Court, 6-4, 6-1, in a match which took just over an hour. Evonne's victory made her the youngest Wimbledon champion since 1962.

Evonne was born on July 31, 1951. Mrs. Goolagong says that "Evonne was squeezing a tennis ball before she was 12 months old, before she learned to walk or talk. Later she would bounce it and catch it and hit it with a broomstick. She was never without it."

Evonne's story as a tennis champion began in Australia's Outback. A hot dry barren region, the Outback takes up three-fourths of Australia's land area.

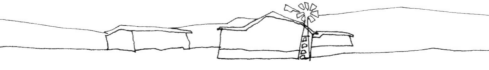

It is a very sparsely settled region. Evonne's home town is Barellan. It is in the state of New South Wales, about 400 miles west of Sydney. Barellan's population is 936, including the 10 members of the Goolagong family. Evonne is the third oldest child.

The Goolagongs are part-Aboriginal. They are the only family in Barellan with an Aboriginal heritage. Ken Goolagong, Evonne's father, has been told that Goolagong means "nose of kangaroo." Mr. Goolagong doesn't know much about his tribal background. So he hasn't been able to share much of the rich Aboriginal history with his children. Evonne knows that she is part-Aboriginal. She knows that her ancestors were the

first residents of Australia. Most of all, Evonne knows that she loves the game of tennis.

It's not unusual for Australians to love tennis. They learned tennis from the British. The British settled Australia, and in 1873 a British army officer, Major Walter Wingfield, invented a form of tennis to be played outdoors on lawns. In time, the Australians became very well known for their tennis interest.

Many of the world's top players have been Australians. The climate in most of Australia is good for tennis and other outdoor sports. The standard of living along the eastern coast, where most Australians live, is good. Children there have lots of time for leisure activities.

People from Australia's Outback, however, have little leisure. And Australians with Aboriginal background have much to overcome. The history of Australia's Aborigines is similar to that of the American Indians. The white man came to Australia about 200 years ago. Through the years the white settler took the natives' tribal lands and crushed their culture. The Aborigines were driven into the western and northern part of the country where the land would not support crops. Thousands of Aborigines died of starvation and sickness.

Today, the Aboriginal race is in danger of extinction. Aborigines are thought to make up less than one-half of one percent of Australia's population. When part-Aborigines are included, the figure is about one percent.

Evonne grew up knowing some of the tragedies of her people. Her parents made every effort to educate their children and encouraged them to pursue their interests.

As a child, Evonne would hang around the local tennis courts and hit the ball against a brick wall with

a bat. At 5, Evonne was serving at a tennis club as a ball girl, running for balls after each play. At 6, Evonne received her first tennis racket from her aunt.

There weren't many 6 year olds waving a tennis racket in Barellan. Evonne loved to hit tennis balls after members of the club had left for the day. Some chickens and some large, bored dogs were her only spectators.

"I used to sleep with that racket my aunt gave me," she says. "Then one day one of my sisters burnt it. I cried for days." But Evonne had already caught the attention of the tennis club's president, Bill Kurtzmann. He gave her another racket. He was the first person to notice Evonne's tennis skill. Bill gave Evonne many pointers on how to play tennis. One day he let her take home an old net. He told her to practice as much as she could on the flat ground near her home.

The Goolagong house is the last one at the end of a bumpy dirt road. Beside their house was a large rectangle of red earth. Mr. Goolagong surrounded the patch with a wire fence. Weeds sprouted all about it. Broken bits of furniture littered it. But the net draped across the middle made it Evonne's tennis court.

When Evonne was 10, Bill Kurtzmann entered her in a tennis tournament in the nearby town of

Narrandera. He took all the Goolagongs along to the event. When they arrived, Bill found that it wasn't a children's contest. It was an adult tournament. It didn't matter. Evonne played and won the women's championship.

That summer a tennis camp came to Barellan. Kurtzmann made sure Evonne was there for lessons. The traveling tennis clinic came all the way from Sydney. It was headed by a man named Vic Edwards.

It was one of Edwards' talent scouts who spotted Evonne. Colin Swan was working in the clinic while Evonne was taking lessons. Evonne surprised him with her skill. He telephoned his boss, Vic Edwards, and asked him to come and look at the girl.

"There is this Aboriginal kid," Colin Swan told Edwards. "She just flows around the court. She is the kind of natural you see once in a long time. She didn't know how to make her shots, of course. But she was always there, in the right place, without even thinking about it."

Vic Edwards drove to Barellan to watch Evonne play. "What do you want to be when you grow up?" Edwards asked Evonne. "I don't know. Maybe a nurse," she told him. "I haven't really thought about it much."

Vic Edwards liked Evonne. He showed her how to position herself for forehand and backhand shots. Then he told her to practice as much as she could with her older brother, Larry. "Next year, I'll come back and I might enter you in a few tournaments," Edwards said.

"Really, I wanted to know if she would stick with it," Edwards said later. "So often it's just a passing interest. I wanted to see if she would keep at it."

Throughout the next 12 months, Evonne did just that.

Edwards found when he returned that Evonne's game had indeed improved. He wanted Evonne to come to his home in Sydney for the summer holidays. These holidays last from Christmas until February in Australia. Mr. and Mrs. Goolagong agreed. With the help of Bill Kurtzmann, Evonne left for the big city. Mr. Kurtzmann had arranged for the Barellan tennis club to buy her a new outfit.

Evonne was a happy person and was quickly liked by everyone she met. She was slim and pretty with bobbing curls. When an adult spoke to her, she would bow her head and speak softly. Though she was shy with adults and strangers, everyone soon saw that Evonne was at ease on the tennis courts.

Vic Edwards liked working with Evonne. He called her backhand volley "a homemade shot." She had taught it to herself by batting the ball against a brick wall. Edwards didn't try to remake it. He just built around it. The thing Edwards remembers most about that first summer with Evonne was her grace around the court. And he recognized that she could hit the ball very hard, always playing it off the center of her racket.

Evonne's tennis game did have some faults.

Concentration is very important in tennis. Sometimes Evonne would let her mind wander, especially when she was playing against someone with less ability. And some say that Evonne is too kind on the courts, that she lacks the killer instinct.

Evonne spent the next 2 summer holidays in Sydney with the Edwards. While Evonne was still 13, she won the under-15 championship in the state of New South Wales. Sydney is the capital of the state. Some tennis coaches said that Evonne had more talent than the leading Australian woman, Margaret Smith, at that age. Margaret, who later married and is now Margaret Court, was the first Australian woman to win the Wimbledon championship.

Vic Edwards knew that Evonne had lots of promise. One day he visited the Goolagongs and asked if he could take Evonne to his home in Sydney to live. Barellan was too small. There wasn't enough encouragement for Evonne to improve the way she needed.

The Goolagongs felt that Mr. Edwards would be very helpful to Evonne. They had always trusted him and so they accepted his idea. The Goolagongs knew that Edwards was giving Evonne a break. Again, the Barellan tennis club bought a new set of clothes for her. And Evonne set off for Sydney, leaving her home town for good.

At the Edwards' home in Sydney, Evonne gained 5 sisters. "At first I was pretty homesick," Evonne said. She knew everyone in Barellan. Sydney seemed so big.

The Edwards gave Evonne a choice of schools—a co-ed school or a private girls school. Since Evonne had always gone to a co-ed school, she chose the girls school. She and one of her Edwards sister, Pat, went to Willoughby Girls school. Evonne thought the school was great fun. She got along especially well with the sports' teachers. And Evonne and Pat Edwards, also an excel-

lent tennis player, became very close friends. It wasn't long before Evonne felt at home.

Vic Edwards felt it was good for Evonne to learn about many things other than playing tennis. For a while it seemed to Evonne that she was spending most of her time studying.

Still Evonne gave a good deal of her time to tennis. Edwards helped Evonne improve her game. Every year for 3 years she won every junior tournament she entered. By 1968, when Evonne was 16, Edwards predicted that she would be the Wimbledon champion in 1974. Evonne would then be almost 23 years old.

In 1970 Evonne won the under-18 Australian championship. That was when Edwards felt Evonne was ready to go overseas. She took her first tour with her coach, Edwards, and her doubles partner, Pat Edwards. She played in England, Holland, France, and Germany. In England, Evonne beat 5 of the world's 10 top-rated women players.

Julie Heldman, an American tennis player, said of her match with Evonne in England in 1970, "I lost a 3-hour match to her. My victory was snatched from me by a flashing backhand which passed me with the force of a cannonball. This stroke and Evonne's ability to cover the tennis court faster than any woman alive have been her strengths."

During her tour of England, Evonne won 3 major tournaments in a row. These wins brought her to Wimbledon. But stepping out onto Center Court at Wimbledon for the first time was too much for her. She lost out with a case of the jitters. Altogether, Evonne won 7 of 21 tournaments she entered that summer.

The next year, 1971, Evonne trained even harder. She was confident and would let no one ruffle her. There was only one person in Australia who had the edge on Evonne. That was Margaret Court. Evonne had always thought of Mrs. Court as her idol. When she was 11, Evonne had her picture taken with Margaret. She had always looked up to Margaret as she was growing up. Now Evonne was about to face her as an equal.

Margaret Court, then 27, was a big winner. In 1970 Mrs. Court had won the Grand Slam—the Wimbledon, French, United States, and Australian women's tennis championships.

Evonne's breakthrough to the top rank of women's tennis came when she faced Margaret Court in the finals of the 1971 French championships in Paris.

Evonne beat Mrs. Court, 7-6, 7-6. Evonne hit her classic backhand down the line with underspin to keep it low. Such shots often left Margaret Court flat-footed. Mrs. Court said that Evonne was willing to hit every ball, even the bad ones. "The harder you hit the ball," Margaret said, "the better she likes it. It's best to slow

the game up, rather than try to outbelt Evonne. And she likes a wide ball. She'll have a crack at anything."

But a few weeks later in the Australian championships, Evonne lost to Mrs. Court. She was leading 5-2, when she got a cramp in her leg. Margaret took advantage of the situation and won the next 11 games.

Vic Edwards was going to wait until 1974 to enter Evonne in as big a tournament as Wimbledon. But when he saw her win the French championships early in 1971, he brought her to Wimbledon that year. Evonne won the women's singles crown and one reporter said, "Overnight, tennis had a cool, hang-loose Cinderella."

A month after the Wimbledon win, Evonne went home to Barellan. The headlines in the newspapers read, "Moochie Is Home." "Moochie" is the Goolagongs' nickname for Evonne. The whole town came out to welcome Evonne. Bill Kurtzmann was the head of the welcome home committee. He took a large autograph book around town and had everyone sign it. Larry Goolagong, Evonne's older brother, painted the house before the occasion. Evonne led the parade through the streets lined with 800 pennants waving "Welcome Evonne/Barellan 1971."

Evonne's two major championships in France and Wimbledon resulted in a top honor for her that year. The Associated Press selected Evonne as the top female athlete in the world in 1971. At home, in January 1972 she was named "Australian of the Year."

Evonne's general athletic abilities have helped

her move to the top ranks of women's tennis. Her speed, coordination, and cool temperament are exceptional.

When summer of 1972 came, Evonne was ready again for Wimbledon. People gathered early in the morning in the London suburb to wait for a chance to get tickets. Evonne moved to the semi-finals. Her opponent was Chris Evert, the teenage United States star. Everyone wanted to see this match. Evonne and Chris are not at all alike, except that both are tennis stars. Evonne is loose. She walked into the Wimbledon courts as she did the year before. Chris walked onto the court with a poker face. Chris knew she had to overcome Evonne's magic with some hard playing.

Evonne was well prepared. But, as always, Evonne's real challenge was concentrating — keeping her mind on the game. Edwards always called that fault of Evonne's "going walkabout." This is the term given to the Aboriginal habit of returning to the bush for a period of time.

The Goolagong-Evert match was like a two-act play. It was alive with feeling, and the audience felt drawn into it. Chris took the lead in Act 1 and won the first set. Her steady play forced Evonne into errors. But instead of "going walkabout," Evonne kept her

poise and concentration. Later, Chris told a reporter, "Her attitude was so good. She was losing, but she never got mad. She was smiling. That's the kind of thing that British crowds love."

And the crowds loved it even more when they saw Evonne snatch the lead away from Chris in Act 2. Evonne hit winners with her backhand and even her forehand. Evonne won 6 straight games and took the second set. Then she got the upper hand in the third set and won it and the match. The applause was wild when Evonne's bright, clear smile seemed to light up the whole stadium as she skipped toward the net. Evonne, flushed and happy, said, "I could feel everyone behind me. It helped a lot." But Evonne couldn't keep her Wimbledon title. Billie Jean King, the 28-year-old Californian, trounced Evonne in the finals 6-3, 6-3. The crowd gave Mrs. King only polite applause. They were disappointed at Evonne's loss. And their silence showed it.

Evonne was in demand despite the loss. She also began making some tours without Edwards. She was becoming more independent. Still shy with strangers, she liked parties and boys. Once she did say though that marriage and tennis didn't seem compatible.

She changed her mind in the summer of 1975. She married Roger Cawley, 25, a London businessman, in Canterbury, England. Vic Edwards was not at the wedding; he was not happy. He had guided Evonne's life for most of 12 years. He also apparently felt that marriage would harm Evonne's tennis career.

Three weeks later, however, Evonne was back at Center Court at Wimbledon. She faced Billie Jean King again for the women's singles title. Mrs. King had said this was her final appearance in singles at Wimbledon.

For Mrs. King, the match was a memorable one. For Evonne, it was one she wanted to forget quickly. Evonne had been playing very well, but she could do nothing right on this day. It was all over in 38 minutes. Evonne won only one game in the 2 sets.

Despite the loss, Evonne Goolagong Cawley at 23 had established herself as a tennis superstar and had become an independent young woman.

JACK NICKLAUS
BILL RUSSELL
MARK SPITZ
VINCE LOMBARDI
BILLIE JEAN KING
ROBERTO CLEMENTE
JOE NAMATH
BOBBY HULL
HANK AARON
JERRY WEST
TOM SEAVER
JACKIE ROBINSON
MUHAMMAD ALI
O. J. SIMPSON
JOHNNY BENCH
WILT CHAMBERLAIN
ARNOLD PALMER
A. J. FOYT

superstars
superstars
superstars

JOHNNY UNITAS
GORDIE HOWE
WALT FRAZIER
PHIL AND TONY ESPOSITO
BOB GRIESE
FRANK ROBINSON
PANCHO GONZALES
LEE TREVINO
KAREEM ABDUL JABBAR
JEAN CLAUDE KILLY
EVONNE GOOLAGONG
ARTHUR ASHE